HAL•LEONARD
INSTRUMENTAL
PLAY-ALONG

AUDIO
ACCESS
INCLUDED

VIOLIN

MANNHEIM STEAMROLLER
Christmas

To access audio visit:
www.halleonard.com/mylibrary

Enter Code
6858-5076-9963-5048

Audio Arrangements by Peter Deneff

ISBN 978-1-4803-9708-8

HAL•LEONARD®
CORPORATION
7777 W. BLUEMOUND RD. P.O. BOX 13819 MILWAUKEE, WI 53213

In Australia Contact:
Hal Leonard Australia Pty. Ltd.
4 Lentara Court
Cheltenham, Victoria, 3192 Australia
Email: ausadmin@halleonard.com.au

Visit Hal Leonard Online at
www.halleonard.com

CONTENTS

BRING A TORCH, JEANETTE ISABELLA

VIOLIN

17th Century French Provencal Carol
Arranged by CHIP DAVIS

GOOD KING WENCESLAS

VIOLIN

Arranged by CHIP DAVIS

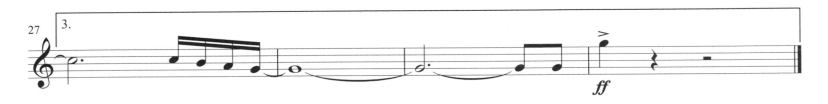

CAROL OF THE BELLS

Ukrainian Christmas Carol
Arranged by CHIP DAVIS

VIOLIN

CHRISTMAS LULLABY

VIOLIN

By CHIP DAVIS

DECK THE HALLS

VIOLIN

Arranged by CHIP DAVIS

GOD REST YE MERRY GENTLEMEN

VIOLIN

19th Century English Carol
Arranged by CHIP DAVIS

GREENSLEEVES

VIOLIN

Sixteenth Century Traditional English
Arranged by CHIP DAVIS

HARK! THE HERALD ANGELS SING

VIOLIN

By FELIX MENDELSSOHN
Arranged by CHIP DAVIS

JOY TO THE WORLD

VIOLIN

Arranged by CHIP DAVIS

PAT A PAN

VIOLIN

Words and Music by BERNARD DE LA MONNOYE
Arranged by CHIP DAVIS

SILENT NIGHT

VIOLIN

Arranged by CHIP DAVIS

TRADITIONS OF CHRISTMAS

VIOLIN

By CHIP DAVIS